Augustine Oteng is a project manager who writes… His work is about poetry and short stories.

He is an innate writer who writes intuitively to excite and inspire. He is fascinated by creative writing, art of rhetoric (literature) and esoteric philosophy. He is a dad of two who lives and works in the UK.

This special dream was inspired by these special family and friends...

Rev. Father Peter O Francis, Seth O Yeboah, Alex Offei, Solomon O Adjei and Michael Kyei

Augustine Oteng

# OTENG'S POEMS: FILES OF WISDOM DIALOGUE

AUSTIN MACAULEY PUBLISHERS™
LONDON • CAMBRIDGE • NEW YORK • SHARJAH

Copyright © Augustine Oteng 2023

The right of Augustine Oteng to be identified as author of this work has been asserted by the author in accordance with sections 77 and 78 of the Copyright, Designs and Patents Act 1988.

All rights reserved. No part of this publication may be reproduced, stored in a retrieval system, or transmitted in any form or by any means, electronic, mechanical, photocopying, recording, or otherwise, without the prior permission of the publishers.

Any person who commits any unauthorised act in relation to this publication may be liable to criminal prosecution and civil claims for damages.

A CIP catalogue record for this title is available from the British Library.

ISBN 9781398466173 (Paperback)
ISBN 9781398466180 (ePub e-book)

www.austinmacauley.com

First Published 2023
Austin Macauley Publishers Ltd®
1 Canada Square
Canary Wharf
London
E14 5AA

A big thanks to the most high…creator of the universe and every individual who contributed to the manifestation of this dream

Cheers x

# Title: The Lost Childhood

Either preachers don't preach
Or they practice not what they preach.
As strong as an ox not to surrender or retreat.
Adamant to be free, I fought fervently to a degree.
To be awarded as sweets to the good kid to handle me as Treats.
For he smiled in a warm welcome to handle me with zeal.

Am smiling in my mirror but he is blind as a bat to me.
Is it better I came clean?
Or should I've been a patience freak;
To elude being a sour salt to be walked on and be crushed
Under life's reckless feet.
Flattened like a chewing gum on a slab in the street
Stuck like a kerb in the Broadway Street,

Reminiscing on the liberty my purblind eyes refuse to see,
Beating my brains out about why the preachers didn't preach
That adulthood is only a larcenist creep
Who sow not what he reaps.

# Title: My Salvation

Salvation, oh my salvation!
I sought diligently for sincere people to lead
Me on this journey but the only choice is to
Do it alone.
For I walk not where their path leads but
Where there's none to create trails out of the
Path of my own
Salvation, oh my salvation!

They inspired me like a lone wolf after I
Enquired but wouldn't walk a step into this
Journey but by myself alone
To balance a thousand tons of awkward loads
Mundane walking life and walk a lonely
Path to discover my lost throne of
Salvation, oh my salvation!

I could wait a million years out of this mortal
Life but on none to transition such a
Destitute soul who bemoans
And long for a perfect regal bearing to be

Crowned upon a splendid royalty of his own.
Salvation, oh my salvation!

For the mirror of the universe emanating me with
Great echo of voice resounding nowhere
But in my ears alone;
A virtue to tame my tongue as quiet as a
Lamb in silence to disregard all vilification for I feel anger.
Yet I rather cease not striving for the
Truth I own to…
Salvation, oh my salvation!

Leaving no stones unturned to carry on in this
Gelid path where the clouds are dark as coal
Yet I scooped it with paper cones
To set flames to the rains to enlighten my feet.
Without a retreat to grab hold of my salvation;
Which is within, yet seems million miles out of reach.
Oh, my salvation!

# Title: Traveller's Diary

My words are my bond to me, myself and I
To voyage any route there is, to the
Unknown destination of comfort where;
The grass is greener at my feet.

I navigate under my own power in the deep
Oceans of rough waters.
I experienced aeroplanes soar through storms
In the highest heights.
A backpacking juvenile peregrinating around
Deserted landscapes and streets of
Suburbs, devoid of life.

My existence as a guttersnipe is though a
Disgust to the sophisticated highly morals.
But what the highly morals say about a
Guttersnipe, says more of him than that of me.
For the voyagers' path is marked by the stars
And not by the dunes of the sand.

I walk a hundred miles each day but in the
Confinements of my cell, going nowhere.

Shedding endless tears in the sleepless nights.
To keep my sanity in the fear of getting deranged from utter Loneliness.
Days turned into weeks and weeks crawled into months,
Then years passed by with comfortless memories and Nightmares.
These are but few battles I refused to bite the dust
But rather bite the bullet to face life as altering adversities Without a repine.
For life is indeed a race, never for the swift but
For those who can actually endure…

# Title: Burning Desires

Fire alarms in my ice castle,
Broken crayons are still colourful but I won't
Break her like she's a pencil.
A perfect intimate affair of the paper and the
Scissors sleekly chiselled,
Rising beautifully in the sky like a rainbow,
Oriented towards the world of broken-hearted
Hills.
Where love evaporates hastily into thin air
With a thrill.
Where the wealthy are affluent yet lacking
Gills.

For some are used at the narcissists' grips in love's guilt.
Yet a pauper in love in such a cold gold-digging world
Has grasped the drill.
Never to let life come between holding his breath till,
This love shines bright like the six-rayed star at all might and
Will.

To lead his groom to the altar for the soul union in the presence of a million

Observers and peepers who're saddened to see the
Old, twisted, same-gender intimacy mill,
Grinding slow but it's grinding still.

# Title: Child's Play

With a submarine in which I delve into the
Belly of the seven seas,
Reaching to the underside of the dull
Bottomless ocean where no man has ever reached.

Where all sea creatures, large and small are
My alter ego beyond carefree.
Their heart pump frequencies of sweet
Symphonies awaiting my return from the moon's fleet,
As an admiral in a one-man army battling a
Million battalions of aliens into defeat.

Before heading to the Oscars where
Countless awards befall my feet,
Ears of deafening silence embrace my speech,
With all the slender ladies cheering to sweep me off my feet.
Ah sweet! Couple of days left to be knighted by Queen Elizabeth before tea.

I couldn't even if I try to hide the greener grass at my feet
Hence a rich kid oft in a candy shopping spree.
For I'm God and time is my masterpiece;

I'm a superhero to hop back in time to rescue the titanic
From getting swallowed by the Atlantic Ocean.
Before I draw blood with my red pen as the best doctor to cure
And free the world from the COVID among other deadly
Diseases.

The best cook with sumptuous banquet, the finest florist with
A lush bunch of the sweetest scented daisies for my lover's
Treat.
For we dine in my multimillion mansion in an invisible
Golden street
Where all these happen in the blink of my mind's eye in sets
Of my inner child's play.

# Title: My Crucifixion

I should have read between the lines to stick to my guns to my
Own decision.
Instead of holding together what must fall apart in dispersion
For less did I reckon people were wrong to disrespect my
Decisions.
Two things I failed to use in my favour;
The intelligence to getting rid of these hot waters and
The wisdom to shunning it out of my direction.
A typical mirage of "To err is human and to forgive is divine".
Instead of being beside myself on the account of erred of
Caution.
Up in arms bent out of shape to lose my cool to cause myself
A calamity of destruction.
Though my nose is kept clean a lifetime, a
Single undeniable atrocity embraces me with a huge
repercussion.
Is this a controlled chaos? My world falling apart?
Or am I leaping into a hasty conclusion?
Once bitten twice shy; to be guilty or not, my chance is slim
Of being impeccable in the eyes of jurisdiction.
In the end,

I must face the music of an eye for an eye and tooth for a tooth—a total crucifixion.

# Title: Empty Wish List

He took her kindness for weakness in her loving breeze of Mists.
Took her seriousness for granted beyond her unreasonable Doubts of wishes
For she wished she was as important as a penalty in a World Cup Final that should never be missed.

She wished you chose her for the tiniest of her perfection Instead of discarding her over the tiniest blemish.
She wished you blow her pains and anxiety away instead of Adding salt to her injuries.

She wished you were her rock, the strong shoulder and the Pillow where she finds serene and heartsease; dethatching From all her emotional shits.
She wished you were the soothing wind under her broken Wings upon which she soars with ease without breaking Sweat like a pregnant fish.
She wished you were by her side in her present, past and Future like time to dispatch all sorrows and hard times in a Lightening swift.

She wished you were a stronghold by her side to shift all the Rough patches into memories of happy endings where all Odds seem like a fragmented rift.
She wished neither fire nor wind,
Birth nor death could move you adrift
But the only wish you granted her is a pair of clipped wings With which she couldn't fly a mile into a journey of a Thousand miles to the land where all wishes come true,
True in reality.

# Title: Experience

Nothing I speak is better than silent
All I fathom is nothing but meaningless
For the lack of learning made my thoughts useless
Absence of knowledge couldn't be the truth of ignorance
But refusing to search to attain it for the betterment of myself
For all the bad things I chose over the good things
I should have done made less sense in the essence of my existence.
Hands of time couldn't be turned back, yet I had no choice
Than to dwell in the past to rearrange to build a pleasant
Today and tomorrow, that's an acceptable purpose of humanity and my coexistence.
Like the grass suffers at the battle of two elephants, so have
I, as a result of denying my mistakes that blundered
Me to fathom a progress with reality of meaninglessness.

# Title: Great Faith

My faith is my crown, my own sole heir
A smile in my frown draws a lot of accolade stares
Blind as a bat, batty clowns see nothing regardless the harder
They stare.
Profound dull starless clouds overrun my narrow stairs
My path runs into rocks to bite the dust in despair
Affrighted wayfarers don't dare where the gypsies get scared
Life foisted with shoddy vales, hills and
Mountains with broken bridges beyond repair.
A growing perpetual gloom and despondence is my inspiration for life
Would be despicable if he has ever been fair
Yet, my hopes and my wishes are intricately entwined on
My faith as a seed that fuels my actions to propel
My fealty to the truth, greater than the wings of an eagle upon
Which I'm soaring there.

# Title: Mirrors

She's the mirror on the wall,
With purblind eyes but sees it all.
From the moment you sneaked through the slightly opened Door,
All the skeletons behind your closet doors,
The secrets you swept under the carpet floors,
Of course, your flaws you blame her faults for
And all her perfect achievements you praised yourself for.
Oh, you silly O.G
When would you grasp her essence behind the scene?
For you fail to sail on her quiescent tides beyond serene.
To save her strength and heart; now frail, shattering into Pieces.
Now you glaring through her eyes as the window to her soul
With awe to see;
All the reflections of the puerile actions you never retreat.
All the vivid lines you refused to read between.
So she hared off behind closed doors,
Praying fervently on the floor,
Like never before,
Begging the universe you would grow wiser and all,
Instead of growing just tall.

# Title: Ode to Moments

As fire never ceases to shine in darkness when lighted
So does a moment never cease to present herself regardless
Plausible or less sacred
For the universe is a lush pie and every bite is a choice of Finest.

As a short journey life is, brimmed with countless moments
In which we co-create our ultimate wish list.
Like the song of the birds are endless in the morning mist.
Moment is the language of the universe spoken in many
Tongues of emotions into attentive ears in our midst
The outermost voice of gratitude wrapped in a veil of Gratefulness
Cherished moments that tickle our fancy to express Thankfulness,
To the uplifting hands of the empathy that stretched forth
Beyond measure of solaces
Moment of thriving joy of gladness
Flourishing with intent to diminish the belting heart of Sadness.
Moment that rekindle the flames of joy to shun the soul from dazedness.

Moment of leap of faith to elevate level of highness.
Like a tossed coin that never perches on its edge,
So does a moment, implausible and absurd.
For he flips to dawn a new era of anguish and distress to offset
All the civility he once showered onto us.
For he is born unestablished,
He's only a tree that bends to the wind of the universe in order
Of present, past and future.

# Title: My Best Friends

My good days are worse than my bad days; that's what my
Friends say.
Oh, fair weather friends of old good days.
Their words are their bond, but I have to go deaf to hear
Vividly every single word they murmur to say.
Actions speak louder, but I have to be blind in order to
Decipher their actions from their deeds each and every single
Day.
In the sunshine we made hays, like a pack of hyenas, we
Laughed out many hooray
Through the good times of delightful sunrays.
What a waste it is when a novice, guided by naiveté, does
Nothing more than deviating from potentials of one's own
Betterment.

A typical fair share of equity, I say.
Knowledge like a garden; it can never be harvested unless it
Is cultivated first to say.
For life is like a shadow and mist passing in a haste
Very short with hardships and trickeries.

But diligence is my master who steers me from my best Friends, who only enjoy my best days to despise my bad Days.
Diligence steers me from my best friends, who in wishing me well
Covet it all for their own sake for now and always.
Oh, fair. Weather friends of old good days!

# Title: Ode to Knowledge

We search in pursuit of knowledge because knowledge is power.

However, unless power could be homologated by certain
Benefice influence with its existence, it can never be
Deemed fit as an output of knowledge.
The delight of the salutary effects of conversant part-takers of
Knowledge is a contrast to the ignorant, whose
Suffering can be quotidian in all aspects of his entire
Lifetime.

Because behind the mightier pen that surpasses the sharpest
Sword is a vast amount of knowledge that peddles it from
The bedrock to the acme of its power.

Nothing is so difficult that knowledge cannot master it.
I'm indeed the womb of every wisdom.
They seek for me in highest planes, yet I'm flooded across plains.
The wise utilise the armours of knowledge to transition the
Destitute and chaotic world into harmony with fearlessness,
Good cheer, tranquillity and peace.

The sophomoric rather employs all the tools of knowledge at His disposal into exploiting and dwindling away the Peaceful world into ruin.

With knowledge in the campaign platform of the cockroach, He descents in the chariots of foxes to prevail over the Kingdom of the chickens.

These specific consequences can be adduced as proof, thus Knowledge embraces every individual beings with open Arms regardless the mindsets.

What do to with knowledge is in our own hands!

# Title: Ode to Motherhood

Does motherhood come with genuine murmuring?
Or was freedom swapped for yawping?
For I'm a flag hanging less stiff but unsure if upright,
Upside down or something?

Tossing and turning unsteady and spiritless waving at nothing.
An Emblemed banner like a pendulum streaming
To and fro in awkward drooping.

Bitten by blistering cold, scorching sun baths my complexion
To the point of melting.
Wind of high spirits keeps me on my toes of flapping
While spells of low winds cast me feebly stuck hanging like
A bandit on a pole of crucifixion

Yet I couldn't bemoan the sorrows in my smiling
I rather keep mum to carry on with my duties to await rewards
Of fruiting

For I'm the captain above board with juggling act to deliver
A safety cruise

Or my tender flowers loll on their stems if I lack water in my cruse.

Like a noon of invisible stars, their bellybuttons hold my
Divine scar, the nucleus from which all nations ever grew
For the myriads of diverse mankind I carry single-handedly
As a one-man crew

Many can be called but only a handful of the few could stand
Tall as strong as an ox to walk in my shoes.
I'm wondering if I'm blowing my horns more than I should
Or only beckoning motherhood less than I should.

# Title: Ode to My Lessons

The lessons learnt are blessed blessings ahead,
The only possession mankind has in common with a bird ensnared.
That makes the two of us.

For her clipped wings are as useless as my legs.
I couldn't be a nimble wit if my lessons were lessened.
For life is a confident trickster with his own implanted lessons
His hash lessons turned out to be blessings in disguise.

But my ears are either perfectly defected to his sole duty of Listening,
Or has he brimmed himself with whatever tickles his fanciness?

Till the lessons set in to tune him to rhythms that spike his
Eardrums to listen with deafening silence.
And all other senses come to their senses as a huddled masses,
Yearning to learn sense from his lyrics of 'causes and Effects'.

For my mind has
His head in the clouds,
My heart followed the crowd to fettered paths,
While my legs jump thousand metres high for those who
Wouldn't walk an inch for me.

A word to the wise wouldn't be enough if he has none in his
Heart to sense that lessons always made sense.

# Title: Ode to the Flute

I couldn't stop staring at the old clock for I'm pondering
Within myself going nowhere worthing. In the dusky depths
Of the cellar, dusty floor and walls know me by name in my
Neighbouring
Stuck in motionless like a bear in hibernation, I explode in my
Head wondering,
As beauty as I am, dreading with awe why do they choose to
Like the ugly over me?
For they rather enjoy the awful tones of the cage birds than
My jaunty symphonies.

My heart pumps the sweetest melodies with silent sounds
Belting my chest with its frequencies.

The only loud whisper I ever make is the sneeze of dusty
Breath to casting myself lucky
Ah! Where are the statured men from the northern constituencies? For my sweet melodies are the offspring of
The warm puff of their lungs in fantasies.

In happy memories of the dazzling moonlight marinated in
The dim star lights among the lilies in love's valley

Where true love is strangely familiar with my sensational
Tunes for which they dance in haste slowly.

Where tall and slender songstresses sing vocals with their
Hearts out along my tunes softly,
With exotic dancers moving their bodies like waves of tides
In their bellies
All to the expense of the essence of my youthful energies.
If only they could be grateful to my tunes of sound they merry.
If only my destitute would make gloomy days for the flutist
Suddenly.

He would lift me up from this loneliness, beautiful as the
Surface of the ocean but no good to sleep on peacefully.

# Title: Reasons and Seasons

Everything happens in seasons.
And everything happens for a reason
Reasons behind seasons and reasons,
Are the reasons why I reason.
One reason why the sun isn't in the season
Of a winter night of action, where he's missing,
Is the same reason the moon longs a lifetime to huggle the
Summer-noon light and kisses.
While the ocean's juicy lips are only meant for the shore's
Coarse sand kisses,
Risen and dazzling diamonds could be falling stars.
Terrific stories behind every scars,
Tenderness and delightful moments behind every smiles,
Orienting like a colourful rainbow across the serene skies.
For the seasons aren't delayed or shy.
But as patient as stone, each awaiting its turn of roles to star.
Frozen winter cold with nippy bites to leaving behind frosty
Scars
Dormant seeds uphold with hopes awaiting
Spring to unfolding their tender stems to reaching the stars.
Autumn's green leaves turned brown,
As the seasonal fake smiles turned into a frown,

All in a wink of dawn.

Dawned on me as I ponder on reasons behind seasons and Reasons, always reasoning along, can barely be drawn.

# Title: Same Difference

Few extra pounds on my flesh repel night standers to attract
My admirers.
Juicy bone is to puppies but eaten by mankind never surprises
Me of their surly mean.
For their preference sake of ideal stature the midget is
Perceived as how an ape cherishes the algebra book,
Yet mathematicians are highly deemed.
Polarity dissolved, gender-twisted men kiss men,
Women kiss women and my thoughts muddled within me.
For it is ridiculously daft of me to descry these as an eyesore
To their dream.
I'm black, dark as coal to light fire into the blue eyes in
Their peachy faces, yet they chose to hate on me.
Till the moon shines in the noon to push the sunshine into the
Midnight, baffled thoughts still flicker at me.

To either fall for the ideologies which brainwash me to choose
From one of their heavens or hells set up before me
Or a fair deal of a grey area to stick to vegetables to eating no
Meat to carry on the reincarnation of me
To and fro, the world where I'm free like a bird,
Yet, other matters are deemed.

Highly in spirits like a kite in the bright blue skies
Yet hold them all in higher esteem
Everything the world evolves around me.

# Title: Shattered

I remember when I lose my mind.
Drifting into millions miles away, leaving the world behind.
As lonely as a cloud shattered beyond bind.
Pondering in the starless dark clouds for a sign.
For both my flimsy shield and compass fails to guard me in
This strangely familiar tides.

And that's all it was; it was a dream, so I sighed.

# Title: Summertime

Running about with my bald, aliened head,
Chasing my sister everywhere in play fight with her skinny
Chicken legs.
We run freely like tireless birds who never perched.
In a torrid blistering heat waves where salt won't melt
But butter doesn't dare.
Running around penniless, a single frosted cone we share.
Drowned in our own perspiration,
Yet we wish it were a cool pool instead.
Our hearts release shattering belts in our chests
Yet, we never rest, for we have been still and calm as a saint
In paradise, awaiting this moment of summer harvest.
Happy as larks the warmer half of the year is
A pond of mud and we are just swines who don't want to see
The end of it in a million years.
Just for own fascinating interest.

# Title: Ode to the Ego

I am Mr Ego; call me Mythomania.
Because I phonied your enlightened self to manifest your
Lower self.

Because my bottomless pit within the lower self is the
Pheromones to attract all the
'If only I had, I would be completely happy and fulfilled'
Into brimming the heart with iniquities and vanities. Because
enough is never enough with me.

Because I seek to usurp your soul by engraving the lamassu
Iconography on the four corners of your heart to blindfold
And incarcerate you into the social matrix.
Because I energised the bull within to stand you out in the
Gullible crowd via a palanquin, seated on shoulders of the
Highly muckety-muck.

Self-conceited and swellheaded lion, devouring, oppressing
And preying on others, all under the influence of power and
Supremacy.

I create you the strongest wings to soar in the highest heights
With none above you like the eagle,
To gaze on the tiniest preys in landscapes far below,
Yet too blind to see the confinements of the matrix
I imprison you right under your nose.

I make you a man of the genius mind with the aptness to
Accumulate galactic sum of dispensable filthy wealth, power
And a materialistic mind kilned into beauteous worth of
Earthly blessings.

After I turned you into a poor benighted soul, I get you drunk
Into oblivion, completely inept to emerge from the
Ego-dominated state of consciousness before conveying you
Into the fathomless abyss, where every effort is futile to save
You from your self-destruction.

# Title: The World Is a Teacher

What was I thinking?
My nose must be stuffed to smell my actions were stinking.
I can't shrink from telling the truth;
Surviving on picking a pocket or two.

As time and tides await no man, so is the fairness of life,
Therefore, I chose not to be fair too.
Though what an old man sees while seated,
Couldn't be seen by a child when standing on a mountain or Stool
For it was a pure supposition on me to climbing the highest Mountain to be clearly visible to the world below.

Nevertheless, my eye gave me a glimpse on life instead.
Life though with her murmur voice but clear to my ears turned
Me into an erudite scholar to govern and judge my own World in diligence.

Often she made me discover little on everyday nous with my Codswallop than my intelligence.
As the bat naps in his own comfort, her tests are prior to her lessons.

He taught me experiences of flames that don't just light up,
But burn with both valuable and bitter lessons.

As the ignorant and the coward are dead before they die,
So are they that are talented ever lived after their death.

# Title: The World's Prayer

Am I a mooncalf not to grieve the afflicted world of decay
And death?

Or with a tenuous grasp on reality of a deafening silence
Among the deaf?

Or purblind to see a one-legged pinky flamingo?
Or could I be a fruitcake to believing her false promise of
Dancing flamenco?

Reality outrun my grip but one thing I never let go
For it is written in my galaxy of fate
But a verse or two to set flames to my faith
"But now,
O Lord, you are our father
We are the clay and you our porter;
And all of us are work of your hands,"

Says Isaiah in Chapter Sixty-four of his book of Verse
Number Eight.
We seek for your will of everlasting might in faith

To cleanse this flu that blemishes our world into a masking face
Purge us, oh God, and free us from this ensnared quarantined cage.
For if Covid-19 is a shepherd's pie,
The world has had an awful bite.
The world is on her knees out of uppity pleading with servile Cry.

# Title: Thyself

There's no evil except for the one you bring to the table!
Thy imagination and mind is capable and more than able;

To attain all good deeds, wishes and anything desirable.
To create reality out of all things that are dreamable and imaginable.

Don't look no further because thyself is within and reachable.
Within thyself all things are possibly achievable.
Get to know thyself!

# Title: Within

I keep searching and searching
Within.
Deeper and deeper
Within
Getting nowhere,
But creepier and creepier,
Making no sense
Within.
But sillier and sillier.
Why the universe never implants us as kindergartener
Within
To be kind and kinder?
Why the gods never impel both youngsters and oldsters
To be showers of love and lovers
within?
Why the kings never coerce us into
Never bowing to the ego so to make this complicated living
Easier,
Within?

# Title: Yesterday Is the Future

Yesterday is the future for today only paved way for the harvest tomorrow.

Tomorrow's reward is indeed the outcome of yesterday's hard work of virtue.
Time at hand isn't important but what one does with it.
For time is only a carriage for whatever a man entrusts him to Deliver.
As it's impossible to arrive at dawn except by path of the night

So shall the day before teaches the day after.
As the farrier's handcrafts doesn't fit his own feet but the Horse's
So are the deeds of yesterday
The major reflection of time yet to come.
For the mystery behind the misery of the sower today is due
To his search of satisfaction in results instead of a satisfaction
In his action of seed sowed yesterday.

Treat yesterday as he is and he remains as he is.
Treat yesterday as though he can and must be and he becomes
What he will and must be in time yet to come.

Only the simple believes the future can't be predicted but the Prudent sees the future like a circle whose centre is a Yesterday and the
Circumference is nowhere but today and tomorrow.
For today betters the good of yesterday to attain the best Tomorrow.
Because future is never alone,
He has a habit of being with yesterday and today.
Believe you me,
That's indeed perfect and a permanent party! Haa!

# Title: Young Love

Our imperfections entwined us perfectly.
For the pair of imperfections traits cancel each other's leaving
Nothing subtly.
Like a calm evening clouds pave way for the moon to dazzle
Shiny.

For her sweet and sour love tingles my tongue to sucking
Keenly.
As the world hails at the kisses of the sun and moon (eclipse)
Delightfully,
So has intimacy embraced us with her warm arms gracefully
For our young love is fitter to hatch than to judge swiftly.

For our young love is fitter to a fulfilment than to rely to
Needless bandy.
For our young love is a hot lava and a friendly fire which
Never cools down easily.
Or else forms a great organised chaos of solid rock upon
Which a temple of love is built diligently,
From generation to generation where our love is celebrated
Cheerfully.

# Title: Insaned Me

I'm sincere, yet I don't trust me.
So lovely, yet I hate me for losing the old sane me.
If I'm innocent, why do I blame me?

For obstructing my own progress to derail me.
I'm as wild as a rebel; so they tamed me.
Like I'm creeping on my imperfections to ashame me.
Within my own highly hope; I phantom a perfect world
Without me.
For I'm only a twisted soul in a good-for-nothing body
Hanging in an unwholesome world really.
For if the world is friendly, why am I so lonely?!
Either my mirrors are gone blur or my eyes are failing me.

A fractured mind to decipher friends from enemies,
Who're careless about the battle before me
Though my hair is washed clean,
My crown is hidden from me.

For each day ahead weighs upon the tons of loads on my head
To shatter my fractured mind like each day is an imprecation
Of affliction upon me.

To sink or to float this deep ocean keeps drifting me,
Far away with no strength and hope to rescue me from me.
I could only be sincere for a helping hand to lead me to the Magical river of sanity to transmute myself into the sane old Me.

# Title: So, I Know

As above, so below.
As the darkness can't overshadow the flimsy flame of a
Candle,
So I know,

Though dull clouds, dark as coal hide the dazzling sun from
Shining on my weariness and sorrow.

He bladed my hair of lair off my head to bare weariness of
Sorrow.
Like I lost my marble to discovering a solace path to follow
Within bald hills and vales where a destitute fox dare to
burrow.

For days of yester years make me lose my mind about Startled
events of tomorrow.
For I'm lost beyond cosmic GPS to follow.

But I'm adamant about the less and less troubles the lion
Could cause the fleas,
So do I know.

# Title: A Place Within

My breath takes me places, places I dare to be.
A place of deafening silence,
A place I talk to me.
A place of million miles away,
A place erratic thoughts lose Track of me.

A place of alpha and beta state, a place implanted within.
A place, scary of becoming the potent of me,
A place of creative me.
A place my inner child come to play,
A place of imaginable me.

A place of magnetic resonance, where good things are Attracted to me.

A place negatives transmute to positive,
A place down within.
A place impossible is visualised possible,
A place of the highest me.

A place of home away from home where all reflections Become reality,
A place down within.

CPSIA information can be obtained
at www.ICGtesting.com
Printed in the USA
LVHW051140070223
738796LV00015B/1856